Creature Comparisons

Frogs

Tracey Crawford

HEINEMANN LIBRARY

www.heinemann.co.uk/library
Visit our website to find out more information about **Heinemann Library** books.

To order:
☎ Phone 44 (0) 1865 888066
📄 Send a fax to 44 (0) 1865 314091
💻 Visit the Heinemann Bookshop at www.heinemann.co.uk/library to browse our catalogue and order online.

First published in Great Britain by Heinemann Library, Halley Court, Jordan Hill, Oxford OX2 8EJ, part of Harcourt Education. Heinemann is a registered trademark of Harcourt Education Ltd.

© Harcourt Education Ltd 2007.
The moral right of the proprietor has been asserted.

Editorial: Tracey Crawford, Cassie Mayer, Dan Nunn, and Sarah Chappelow
Design: Jo Hinton-Malivoire
Picture Research: Tracy Cummins, Heather Mauldin, and Ruth Blair
Production: Duncan Gilbert

Originated by Chroma Graphics (Overseas) Pte. Ltd
Printed and bound in China by South China Printing Company

10 digit ISBN 0 431 18228 0
13 digit ISBN 978 0 431 18228 5

11 10 09 08 07
10 9 8 7 6 5 4 3 2 1

British Library Cataloguing in Publication Data
Crawford, Tracey
  Frogs. - (Creature comparisons)
  1.Frogs - Juvenile literature
  I.Title
  597.8'9
A full catalogue record for this book is available from the British Library.

Acknowledgements
The publishers would like to thank the following for permission to reproduce photographs: Corbis pp. **4** (monkey, Frank Lukasseck/zefa; bird, Arthur Morris), **10** (B. Borrell Casals; Frank Lane Picture Agency), **11** (Michael & Patricia Fogden), **12** (Michael & Patricia Fogden), **14** (Michael & Patricia Fogden), **15** (Joe McDonald), **16** (Joe McDonald), **18** (Michael & Patricia Fogden), **22** (poison arrow frog, Paul A. Souders; tree frog, SIE Productions/zefa; Horned frog, Michael & Patricia Fogden), **23** (frog with webbed feet, Michael & Patricia Fogden); Getty Images pp. **4** (fish), **6** (Christoph Burki), **8** (George Grall), **17** (Heinrich van den Berg), **19** (Frank Greenaway), **23** (tadpoles, George Grall); Michele Menegon p. **9**; Carlton Ward pp. **4** (snake), **5**, **13**, **20**, **21**.

Cover photograph of a blue poison arrow frog reproduced with permission of Nature Picture Library/Ingo Arndt and a common frog reproduced with permission of NHPA/Jordi Bas Casas. Back cover photograph of a big frog reproduced with permission of Corbis/Joe MacDonald.

Every effort has been made to contact copyright holders of any material reproduced in this book. Any omissions will be rectified in subsequent printings if notice is given to the publishers.

Contents

There are many types of animals.

Frogs are one type of animal.
Frogs are amphibians.

All frogs can swim.

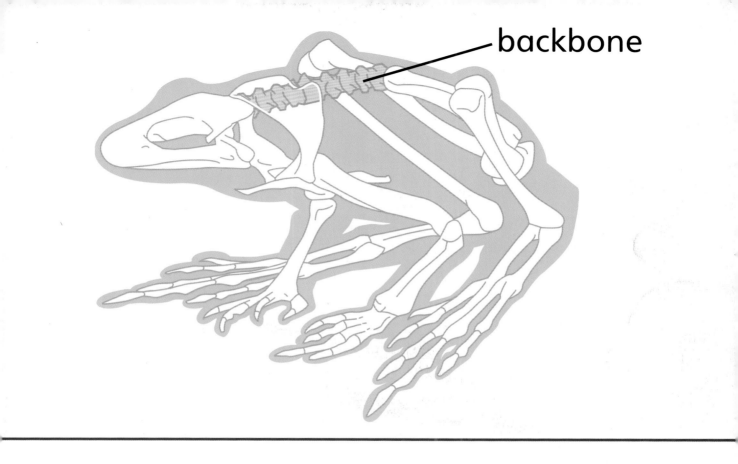

backbone

All frogs have a backbone.

Most frogs hatch from an egg.

But this frog does not.

tadpole – baby frog

Most baby frogs are tadpoles.
Tadpoles have a tail.

These baby frogs are not tadpoles.
They do not have a tail.

Most frogs have wet skin.

But this frog does not.

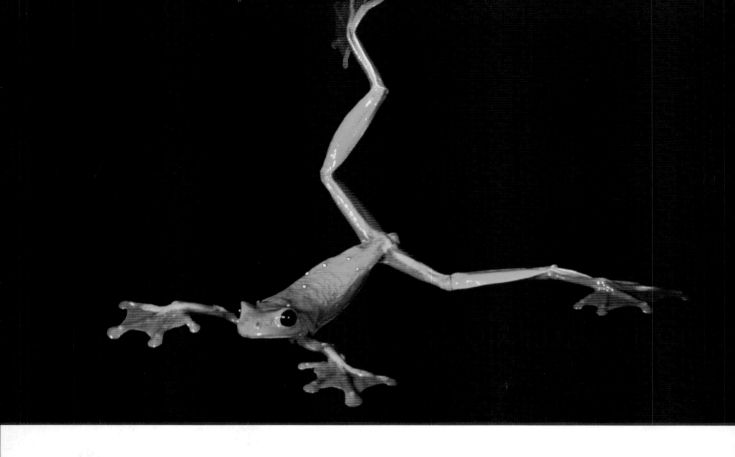

Some frogs have webbed feet.

But this frog does not.

Some frogs are big.

Some frogs are small.

Some frogs have spots.

Some frogs have stripes.

Every frog is different.

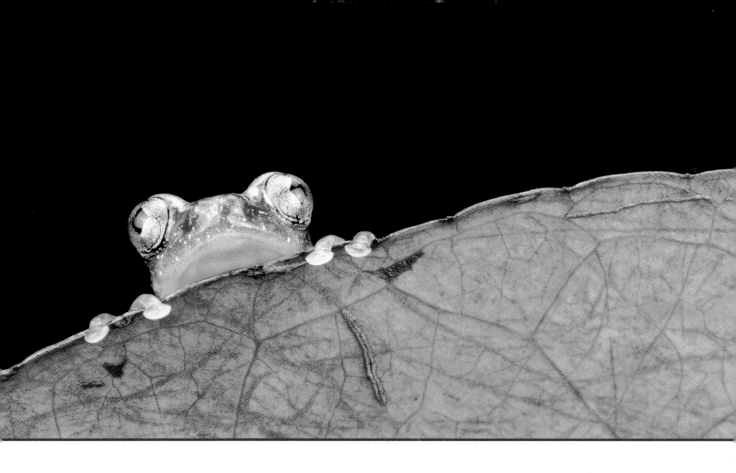

Every frog is special.

Frog facts

Some frogs have poison in their skin. These frogs can be brightly coloured.

This frog looks like leaves on the ground. This helps it hide.

Some frogs can puff out their neck like a balloon. This helps them sing.

Picture glossary

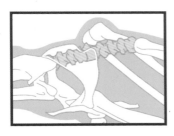 **backbone** the part of the skeleton that goes from the head to the bottom

 **hatch** to be born from an egg

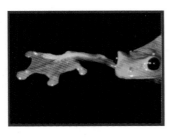 **webbed** having toes or fingers that are joined together

Index

Notes to parents and teachers
Before reading
Talk to the children about frogs. Have they ever seen one in a pond? Explain that frogs are amphibians, which means they are creatures that can live in water and on land.

After reading
Talk to the children about the lifecycle of most frogs from frogspawn to tadpoles to young frogs.
Sing the song: "Five little speckled frogs, Sat on a hollow log, Eating some most delicious bugs. (Yum Yum!) One jumped into the pool, Where it was nice and cool. Then there were four green speckled frogs. (Croak Croak!)"
Make a paper frog puppet: You will need a sheet of A4 thin green card. Fold it into thirds. Fold in half then fold in half again. Form into a "W" shape. Draw eyes on the front. Add a tongue made from red paper and glue inside the upper fold of the "W". Put a thumb in the lower "jaw" and fingers in the upper "jaw". Now you have a wide-mouthed frog!

Titles in the *Creature Comparisons* series include:

Hardback   0 431 18226 4

Hardback   0 431 18225 6

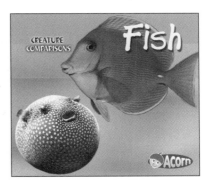

Hardback   0 431 18224 8

Hardback   0 431 18228 0

Hardback   0 431 18223 X

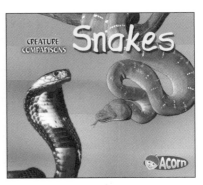

Hardback   0 431 18227 2

Find out about other titles from Heinemann Library on our website www.heinemann.co.uk/library